SCHOLASTIC

ENGLISH SKILLS

Spelling and vocabulary

Workbook

Ages 8–9

SCHOLASTIC

ENGLISH SKILLS

Spelling and vocabulary

Scholastic Education, an imprint of Scholastic Ltd
Book End, Range Road, Witney, Oxfordshire, OX29 0YD
Registered office: Westfield Road, Southam,
Warwickshire CV47 0RA

www.scholastic.co.uk

© 2016, Scholastic Ltd

1 2 3 4 5 6 7 8 9   6 7 8 9 0 1 2 3 4 5

British Library Cataloguing-in-Publication Data
A catalogue record for this book is available from the British Library.

ISBN 978-1407-14190-9
Printed by Ashford Colour Press

Due to the nature of the web we cannot guarantee the content or links of
any site mentioned. We strongly recommend that teachers check websites
before using them in the classroom.

Every effort has been made to trace copyright holders for the works
reproduced in this book, and the publishers apologise for any inadvertent
omissions.

Author
Pam Dowson

Editorial
Rachel Morgan, Anna Hall, Jenny Wilcox, Red Door Media

Design
Neil Salt and Nicolle Thomas

Cover Design
Nicolle Thomas

Illustration
Dave Smith/Beehive Illustration

Cover Illustration
Eddie Rego

Contents

4 | INTRODUCTION
How to use this book

5 | CHAPTER 1
Revisit and reinforce

26 | CHAPTER 2
Prefixes

35 | CHAPTER 3
Suffixes and word endings

48 | CHAPTER 4
Possession

57 | CHAPTER 5
Building knowledge

69 | CHAPTER 6
Applying and using knowledge

80 | PROGRESSION
Progress chart

How to use this book

- *Scholastic English Skills Workbooks* help your child to practise and improve their skills in English.

- The content is divided into topics. Find out what your child is doing in school and dip into the practice activities as required.

- Keep the working time short and come back to an activity if your child finds it too difficult. Ask your child to note any areas of difficulty. Don't worry if your child does not 'get' a concept first time, as children learn at different rates and content is likely to be covered at different times throughout the school year.

- Check your child's answers at www.scholastic.co.uk/ses/spelling.

- Give lots of encouragement, complete the 'How did you do' for each activity and the progress chart as your child finishes each chapter.

Activity title
The title of the activity.

Instruction
The instruction tells you what to do.

How did you do?
Colour in Ollie Owl with a ✔ if you could do the activity. Colour in Ollie Owl with a ? if you need help or more practice.

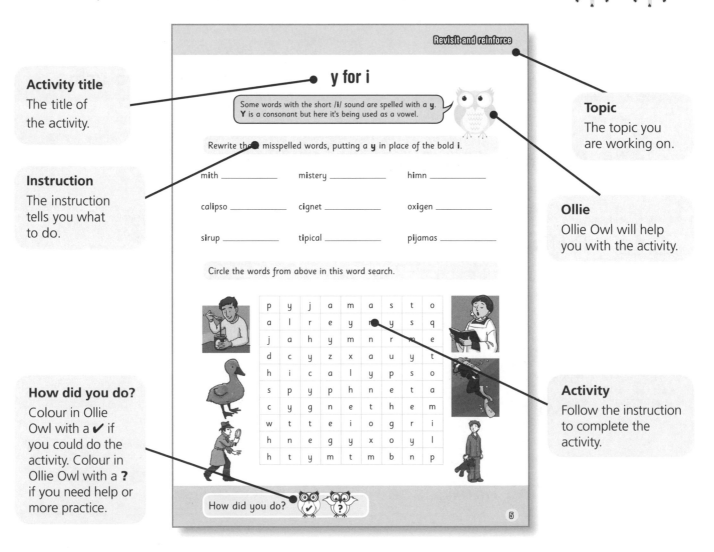

Topic
The topic you are working on.

Ollie
Ollie Owl will help you with the activity.

Activity
Follow the instruction to complete the activity.

If you need help, ask an adult!

y for i

Some words with the short /i/ sound are spelled with a **y**.
Y is a consonant but here it's being used as a vowel.

Rewrite these misspelled words, putting a **y** in place of the bold **i**.

m**i**th _____

m**i**stery _____

h**i**mn _____

cal**i**pso _____

c**i**gnet _____

ox**i**gen _____

s**i**rup _____

t**i**pical _____

p**i**jamas _____

Circle the words from above in this word search.

p	y	j	a	m	a	s	t	o
a	l	r	e	y	n	y	s	q
j	a	h	y	m	n	r	m	e
d	c	y	z	x	a	u	y	t
h	i	c	a	l	y	p	s	o
s	p	y	p	h	n	e	t	a
c	y	g	n	e	t	h	e	m
w	t	t	e	i	o	g	r	i
h	n	e	g	y	x	o	y	l
h	t	y	m	t	m	b	n	p

How did you do?

Fill the gaps

Fill in the gaps in the extract below, using the words in the box.

| lyrics   hymn   calypso   typical   symbols   mystery   system |

To many of us, the _____ used to write down musical

notes are a _____. But to songwriters and musicians

they are essential tools. A _____ piece of sheet music,

such as that for a _____ sung in church, will also

include the _____ to be sung. Some types of tunes,

for example a tricky Caribbean _____ rhythm, are

especially difficult to read. But the _____ for musical

notation can be understood whatever language you speak.

Write sentences for each of these **y** words.

pyjamas _____

_____

gym _____

_____

syrup _____

_____

Egypt _____

_____

How did you do?

How do you say ou?

In some words, **ou** makes a short /u/ sound, such as in the word **young**.

Write these **ou** words in alphabetical order. Where the first few letters are the same, use the second or third letter to put them in order.

double   _____

cousin   _____

couple   _____

enough   _____

courage   _____

nourishment   _____

rough   _____

touch   _____

Choose from the words to complete these sentences.

1. The soldier showed great _____ in the battle.

2. After eating four doughnuts, Fred said, 'That's _____!'

3. Driving the wrong way up a one-way street will get you in
    _____.

4. I prefer to live in the _____ rather than the city.

5. Food provides our bodies with _____ to survive.

How did you do?

Word sort

Sort these **ou** words into the correct shape. Write words where **ou** sounds like a short /**u**/ in the moustache. Write words where **ou** sounds like /**ow**/ in the cloud.

count   country   encourage   south   southern   flourish
roundabout   trouble   couple   foundation   doubt

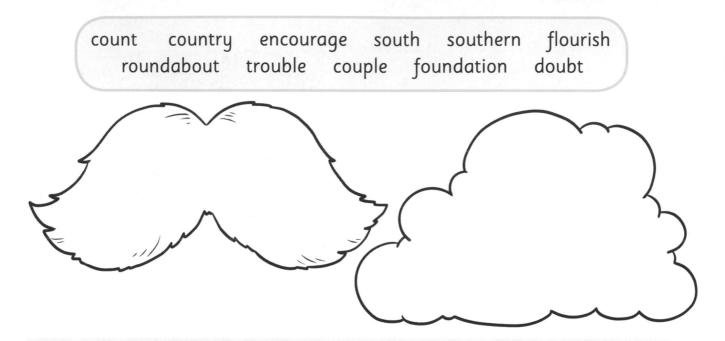

Work out what these **ou** words are and put in the missing vowels. Then write the complete words.

1. —nc— —r—g—   _____

2. c— —s—n   _____

3. d— —bl—   _____

4. y— —ng—r   _____

5. t— —ch—ng   _____

6. c— —ple   _____

How did you do?

Solve the clues

The /**ai**/ sound can be spelled **ei**, **eigh** and **ey,** as in **vein**, **weight** and **obey**.

Solve these clues. All the answers are words with the /**ai**/ sound in them. Some are spelled with **ei**, some with **eigh** and some with **ey**.

1. A noise made by a horse. _____

2. Someone living next door. _____

3. A number that is 2 less than 10. _____

4. A woman's face or head covering. _____

5. What predators hunt and eat. _____

6. Miss Muffet ate this with curds. _____

7. Dieting makes you lose this. _____

8. To do as you are told. _____

9. Use it to travel on snow. _____

10. Blood travels round your body in these. _____

11. A dull colour, made by mixing black and white paint. _____

Compare your answers with those of a friend. Then check your spellings in a dictionary.

How did you do?

Look closely

Write the example words in the correct boxes below. Look up any unfamiliar words in the dictionary.

> vein   neigh   beige   drey   reign   sleigh   weight
> convey   veil   eighty   neighbours

Seven nouns	
Two words you might use in maths	
The word that is a colour	
The plural	
The word with three vowels	
The word with four vowels	
The word with one vowel	
Two adjectives	
Four verbs	

Solve these tricky anagrams! The answers all contain **ei**, **eigh** or **ey**.

1. bonier hug _____ (a person who lives next door)

2. the genie _____ (a number)

3. being yo _____ (doing what someone says)

How did you do?

k or sh?

The letters **ch** can make a /**k**/sound, such as in the word **echo**, and a /**sh**/ sound, as in the word **chef**.

Sort these words according to their sound and write them in the correct window.

choir   quiche   chic   orchid   scheme   chandelier   brochure
character   anchor   Charlotte   orchestra   parachute   chorus
pistachio   stomach   Christopher   chateau   Christmas

Chemist

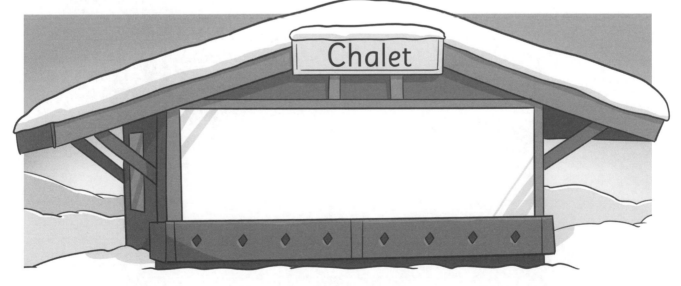

Chalet

How did you do?

Word and picture match

Choose the word that matches the picture. Below each picture, write a sentence that uses the word.

anchor   chef   quiche   choir   orchestra   moustache

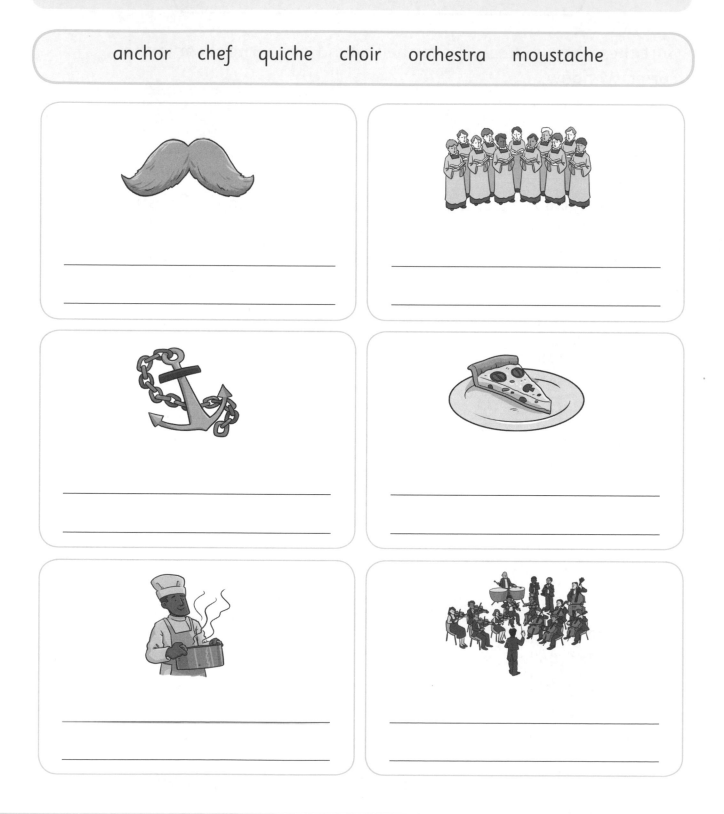

How did you do?

Silent c

In these words, the **c** after the **s** is silent, so the sound is /**s**/. For example **scene** sounds like **seen**.

Write the words from the wordbank beside their meanings.

scimitar   scientist   scissors   ascend   descend
crescent   muscles   adolescent   fascinated

1. You cut with these. _____

2. A teenager. _____

3. Part of the body. _____

4. To go up. _____

5. A curved shape. _____

6. Someone who studies science. _____

7. To go down. _____

8. Very interested in and absorbed by. _____

9. A curved sword. _____

Look up these **sc** words in a dictionary and write their meanings.

10. disciple _____

11. scenic _____

How did you do?

Silly sentences

Remember that **sc** makes the /**s**/ sound in these words.

Some of the words below are spelled correctly and some are incorrect. Circle the incorrect ones, then write the correct spellings underneath.

fasinated   abscess   dicipline   ascent
decend   senery   scientific

_____   _____   _____   _____

Use the words above and those in the wordbank below to make up some silly sentences. Try to use some words that begin with the same sound. You can use words more than once. There is an example to help you.

scissors   science   scientist   crescent   scented
fascinating   muscles   adolescent   scimitar   scene

Example: Steve the silly scientist was secretly fascinated by scented scissors.

_____

_____

_____

_____

_____

_____

How did you do?

Tricky endings

Sort these words by putting the **que** words in the Word Boutique and the **gue** words in the meringue.

In these words, **que** is pronounced /**k**/ and **gue** is a hard /**g**/ as in **gum.**

unique   dialogue   league   cheque   tongue   mosque
fatigue   antique   plague   plaque   colleague

Word Boutique

meringue

Match the words to their meanings by drawing a line between them.

Extreme tiredness   monologue

Part of the mouth   colleague

Someone you work with   fatigue

A speech by one person   mosque

A place of worship   tongue

How did you do?

Working with letters

In these words, every other letter is missing. Complete the spellings by putting in the missing letters then write the whole word.

1. anti____u____   _____

2. collea____u____   _____

3. che____u____   _____

4. merin____u____   _____

5. ton____u____   _____

6. uni____u____   _____

All these words end with **que** or **gue**.

Solve the clues and write the words.

7. Old and valuable object. _____

8. Light sugary cake made from egg whites. _____

9. The muscular organ in the mouth. _____

10. Piece of paper used in place of cash. _____

11. Being the only one of its kind. _____

12. One of a group of people that work together. _____

How did you do?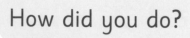

Recapping prefixes

The prefixes **dis** and **mis** make words into their opposites.

Write **dis** or **mis** to make these words opposite.
Then write the new words on the lines.

1. _____appeared   _____

2. _____fortune   _____

3. _____taken   _____

4. _____organised   _____

5. _____understood   _____

6. _____appointment   _____

Choose words from above to complete the sentences.

7. This is a mess! You are so _____.

8. The spy went wrong as he had _____ the message.

9. It was a big _____ to have no birthday presents.

10. Because of the sunshine, the snow had _____.

11. It was my _____ to choose the wrong queue.

12. Sorry, you're _____. You have the wrong number.

How did you do?

More prefixes

Choose the prefix **anti** or **super** to complete these words, then write the words in the shapes. Use a dictionary to find other words with these prefixes and add them to the boxes.

_____biotic   _____sonic   _____charged

_____septic   _____market   _____climax

Anti	Super

In the word list below, circle the words with prefixes.

dismiss   missed   antic   superb   regroup   autopilot

discuss   miscalculate   reached   disarm   mission

real   antiques   disappointed   rerun   impress

How did you do?

Mix and match

Add the correct prefix to the words below. Choose from **re**, **dis**, **mis**, **super**, **anti**, **auto**. Then write the new words.

1. _____ biotic   _____
2. _____ comfort   _____
3. _____ ordered   _____
4. _____ clockwise   _____
5. _____ mobile   _____
6. _____ consider   _____
7. _____ courage   _____
8. _____ vision   _____
9. _____ approve   _____
10. _____ judge   _____
11. _____ sonic   _____
12. _____ understand   _____
13. _____ agree   _____
14. _____ freeze   _____

Endings starting with vowels

Add **ing**, **er** and **ed** to the root words.

1. add _____ _____ _____

2. cool _____ _____ _____

3. help _____ _____ _____

4. jump _____ _____ _____

Add **ing**, **er** and **ed** to these root words, but double the final consonant first.

5. shop _____ _____ _____

6. plan _____ _____ _____

7. quiz _____ _____ _____

8. travel _____ _____ _____

Add **ing**, **er** and **ed** to these root words, but drop the final **e** first.

9. use _____ _____ _____

10. move _____ _____ _____

11. care _____ _____ _____

12. save _____ _____ _____

How did you do?

Practise your suffixes

Add **en** to these root words, then write the new words.

1. sick_____   _____

2. soft_____   _____

3. quick_____   _____

4. length_____   _____

5. strength_____   _____

6. sharp_____   _____

7. stiff_____   _____

Add **en** to these words, changing the root word first. Explain how you changed the root word.

Root word	How to change it	New word
wide		
forgot		
forbid		
mistake		

Write sentences using four of the new words you have made.

_____

_____

_____

_____

How did you do?

Choose the suffix

Write new words by adding suffixes to the root words.
Remember, you might need to change some of the root word first.

You can't add all the
suffixes to all the words.

Root word	en	er	ed	ing
cancel				
limit				
model				
fast				
choose				
forbid				
kidnap				
prefer				
video				
broad				
finish				
adventure				
bounce				
slip				
stare				

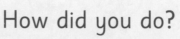 How did you do?

Adding ly

Change these adjectives to adverbs by adding **ly**. Write the full word.

Adding **ly** changes an adjective to an adverb, for example, slow – slowly.

glad _____   loud _____

careful _____   beautiful _____

When the root word ends in a **y**, we change it to **i** before adding **ly**, for example, happy – happily.

Change these in the same way.

angry _____   lazy _____   handy _____

easy _____   sleepy _____   noisy _____

Write the adverbs made by adding **ly** to these adjectives. Think about the endings!

sudden _____   steady _____   necessary _____

nice _____   practical _____   busy _____

Circle the adjectives below that could be made into adverbs by adding the suffix **ly**. Write the adverbs underneath.

useless   weary   big   sad   yellow   old   creepy

desperate   excited   wooden   terrified

_____   _____   _____   _____

How did you do?

23

More ly

When we add **ly** to words ending in **le**, we drop the final **e** first.

Change these adjectives to adverbs. The first one has been done for you.

simple simply   humble _____   noble _____

sensible _____   gentle _____   bubble _____

giggle _____   prickle _____

When an adjective ends in **ic**, we must add **ally** to change it into an adverb.

Change these adjectives to adverbs. The first one has been done for you.

music musically   magic _____   comic _____

tragic _____   aerobic _____   heroic _____

athletic _____   organic _____

Choose one of the adverbs to complete the sentences.

1. He stroked the cat _____, making it purr.

2. When she was tickled, she became very _____.

3. We like to grow our vegetables _____ with no chemicals.

4. Cinderella's rags were _____ transformed.

How did you do?

Are you sure?

Add **sure** or **ture** to complete the words. When you've finished, check your spellings in a dictionary and tick the ones you got right.

punc_____   pres_____   na_____   trea_____

crea_____   mois_____   furni_____   enclo_____

depar_____   plea_____   sculp _____   tex_____

Find and circle these words in the word search.

measure   future   signature   leisure   picture   insure
vulture   exposure   temperature   mixture

t	e	m	p	e	r	a	t	u	r	e
e	r	i	i	l	e	w	i	o	s	r
s	u	x	c	r	m	x	d	f	e	u
t	t	t	t	i	n	s	u	r	e	t
u	l	u	u	k	i	t	r	s	u	u
r	u	r	r	h	w	l	p	i	t	f
e	v	e	e	x	p	o	s	u	r	e
s	t	e	r	u	s	a	e	m	s	u
l	e	i	s	u	r	e	i	t	u	r
a	e	r	u	t	a	n	g	i	s	c

How did you do?

The prefix sub

The prefix **sub** means **under**.

Choose words from the sea that can have the prefix **sub** added to them. Write the words in the submarine.

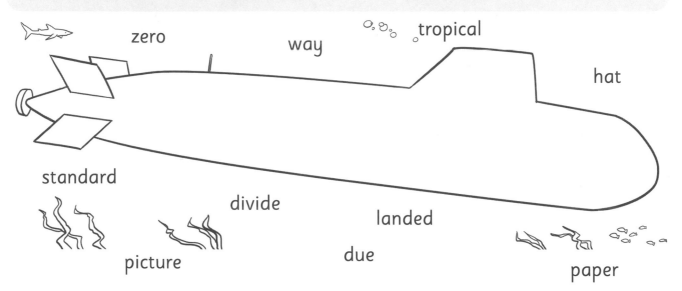

zero   way   tropical

standard   hat

divide   landed

picture   due   paper

Choose words from the submarine to match the meanings. Write the word next to its meaning.

1. Not up to the expected quality. _____

2. Extremely low temperature. _____

3. Passageway under the road. _____

4. Split into pieces. _____

5. Calm down. _____

6. Warm sunny climate. _____

How did you do?

The prefix inter

The prefix **inter** means between or among. Sometimes it's added to letter strings that are not words – like **cept**, **fere**, and **rupt**.

Add the prefix **inter** to each word then write the complete word.

_____ active   _____   _____ fere   _____

_____ national   _____   _____ locked   _____

_____ rupt   _____   _____ school   _____

_____ cepted   _____   _____ view   _____

Choose the right **inter** words to complete the sentences.

1. We won the trophy at the annual _____ quiz.

2. He had an _____ for the job.

3. It's bad manners to _____ when someone is speaking.

4. The guided missiles _____ the attacking rockets.

5. Wales played Scotland in the _____ rugby match.

6. I enjoy playing _____ games on my computer.

7. It's not a good idea to _____ when Dad's cooking!

8. The metal loops had been _____ to make a chain.

How did you do?

Sub or inter?

Add **sub** or **inter** to each word. Write the **sub** words under the ground and the **inter** words between the walls.

> freezing   mix   heading   act   aqua   galactic
>
> committee   merge   Arctic   lace   change   net

Write sentences that include four words with the prefixes **sub** or **inter**.

_____

_____

_____

_____

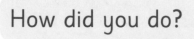

How did you do?

Two uses of in

The prefix **in** has two meanings – it means both **not** as in 'incorrect' and **in** as in 'inside'.

Sort the words according to the meaning of the prefix.

include   inaccurate   involve   inwards   into   insecure
inject   install   invisible   inexpensive   incredible
inexperienced   inspire   inflexible   incomplete

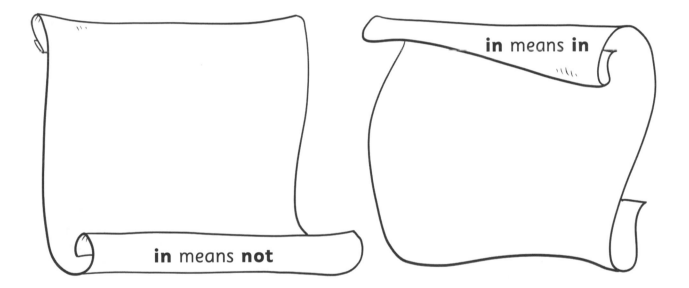

in means **in**

in means **not**

Look up these words in a dictionary and write their meanings.

1. inability _____

2. incision _____

3. infested _____

4. insert _____

5. inappropriate _____

How did you do?

Making opposites

The prefixes **im**, **il** and **ir** make opposites when they are added to a root word. If the root word begins with **l**, we add **il**. If it begins with **m** or **p**, we add **im**. If it begins with **r**, we add **ir**.

Add the correct prefix to the root words, then write the new words.

1. _____practical   _____

2. _____literate   _____

3. _____responsible   _____

4. _____reparable   _____

5. _____measurable   _____

6. _____mobile   _____

7. _____legal   _____

8. _____regular   _____

Circle the words with the wrong prefixes. Write the correct words below.

inpossible   illogical   inperfect   ilmoveable   imreplaceable

irrelevant   inpolite   imperfect   impatient   imresistible

_____   _____

_____   _____

_____   _____

How did you do?

Prefix recap – dis, mis, re

Underline the words with the wrong prefix. Write the correct words in order, under the paragraph.

At first, we were misappointed when we realised we had distaken the breed of our new puppy. We thought we would misturn it to the breeder, but we soon recovered that the breed didn't matter – we quickly fell in love with Frodo. Even though he would misappear and get into dischief, he was still fun to have around. He would run until he was exhausted, then sit wagging his tail until he miscovered. It would have been a big retake to misplace that little pup!

_____   _____   _____

_____   _____   _____

_____   _____   _____

Choose the correct prefix – **dis**, **mis** or **re** – for the words below, then write the whole word next to it.

1. _____appear   _____

2. _____connect   _____

3. _____fortune   _____

4. _____honest   _____

5. _____claim   _____

6. _____lead   _____

How did you do?

Prefix recap – super, anti, auto

Add the correct prefix to these words and write them in the shapes. Some words may fit into more than one category.

graph   highway   climax   correct   sonic   human
biography   freeze   biotic   visor   septic   static   mobile
intend   power   social   hero   clockwise   pilot   bug

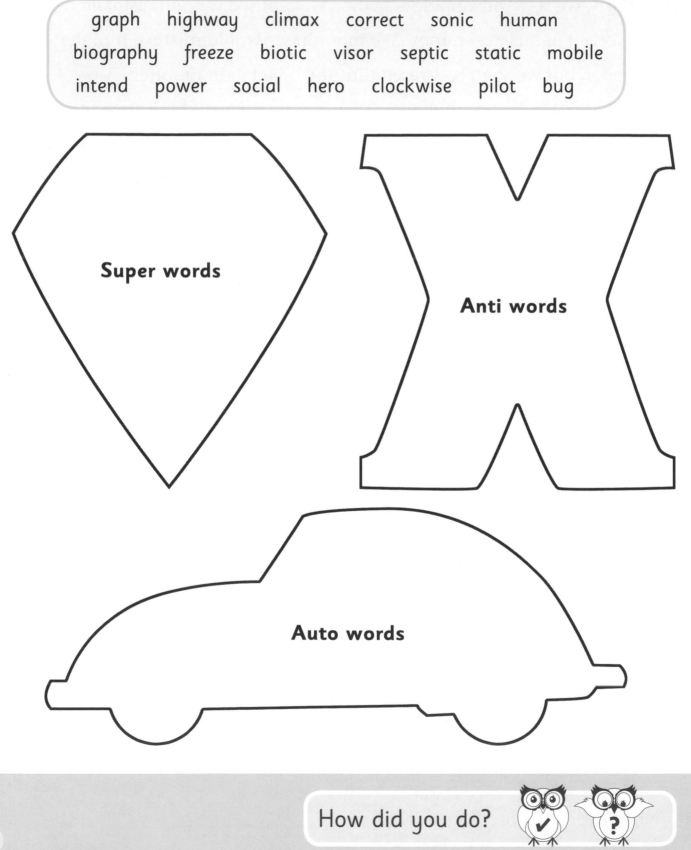

Super words

Anti words

Auto words

How did you do?

Prefix recap – sub, inter

Complete the words in the sentences. All the words have the prefix **sub** or **inter**.

1. The heavy snow ___n___e___f__r___d with our journey.

2. ___u__t__a__t___o___ is the opposite of addition.

3. A news flash ___n__e__r__p__e___ the television programme.

4. The new ___u___m___r___n___ can dive deeper than any before it.

5. The astronauts headed for the ___n__e__n__t__o___a___ space station.

6. The builders' ___u__s__a__d__r___ work was unacceptable.

7. Tomorrow is the ___n__e__s__h__o___ hockey match.

8. I don't like to ___u__m__r__e my head in cold water.

9. I'm getting better at using ___u__h__a__i__g___ in my non-fiction writing.

Write the words you found below.

_____

_____

_____

_____

How did you do?

Prefix recap – in, il, im, ir

Choose the best prefix for these words. Write each word in the correct section of the circle.

mobile   regular   visible   legal   credible   crease   literate

possible   resistible   expensive   logical   measurable

accurate   responsible   practical   polite   secure   perfect

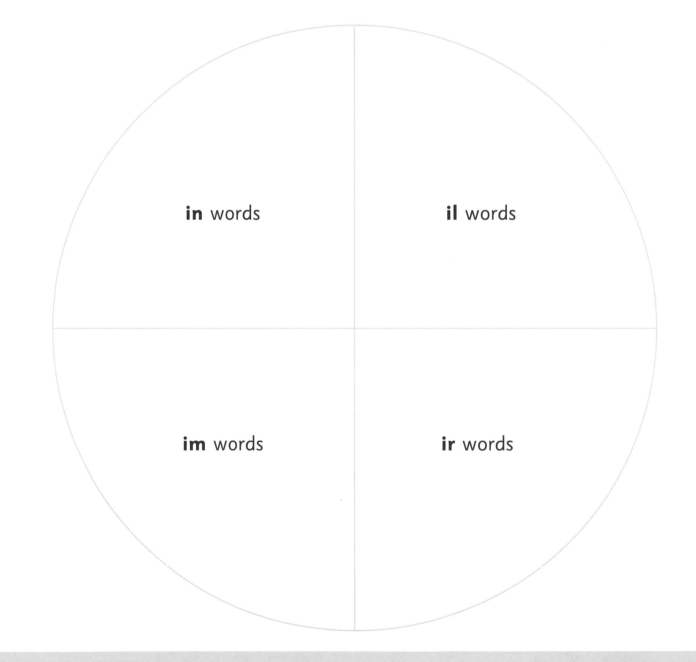

in words

il words

im words

ir words

How did you do?

The suffix ation

Write the nouns formed when you add **ation** to these verbs.

inform _____ adapt _____ found _____

Change these verbs by dropping the final **e** before adding **ation**.

fascinate _____ examine _____ hibernate _____

Change these words by missing out the **i** and adding **ation**.

explain _____ exclaim _____ proclaim _____

Change these words by replacing **y** with **i** before adding **cation**.

classify _____ magnify _____ multiply _____

Use the rules above to help you add **ation** to these words.

relate _____ tempt _____ illustrate _____

apply _____ saturate _____ destiny _____

Use a dictionary to check all your spellings.

How did you do?

ous endings

ous means full of.

Add the suffix **ous** to the root words.

thunder_____   poison_____   venom_____   danger_____

Match these root words to their **ous** word by drawing a line between them.

glamour	famous
humour	numerous
fame	nervous
ridicule	glamorous
disaster	glorious
nerve	humorous
number	marvellous
marvel	ridiculous
glory	disastrous

Write the matching pairs of words below.

_____

_____

_____

_____

How did you do?

36

The suffixes ation and ous

Write the root words below in the shapes, adding either the suffix **ation** or the suffix **ous**. Change the spelling of the root word if you need to.

expect   glory   navigate   adventure   courage   miracle   form
create   admire   carnivore   disaster   irritate

ation   **ous**

Choose **ation** or **ous** words from above to complete the sentences below. The first letter is given to help you.

1. The sculpture was a wonderful c_____.

2. C_____ animals are those that eat meat.

3. Before GPS, we had to use maps for n_____.

4. An itchy rash causes great i_____.

5. The brave mountaineer had an a_____ character.

How did you do?

Endings that sound like /shun/

We spell the /**shun**/ sound in different ways – **tion**, **sion**, **ssion**, **cian**.

Sort the words into the right boxes.

tension   magician   direction   expression   technician   education   electrician   imagination   admission   optician   subtraction   operation   suspension   politician   permission   injection

tion words: these are the most common

cian words: these are usually jobs

sion words: there aren't many of these

ssion words: these are usually nouns

How did you do?

More /shun/ words

Look at how the root words change when **sion** or **tion** is added.

> extend – extension   act – action   pretend – pretension
>
> except – exception   confuse – confusion   frustrate – frustration
>
> tense – tension   educate – education

Write rules to help you know which ending to use.

If a word ends in_____, we should_____.

If a word ends in_____, we should_____.

Use your rules to add **sion** or **tion** to these root words, writing out the new word in full.

expand	suspense
_____	_____
complete	invent
_____	_____
comprehend	quest
_____	_____
decorate	hibernate
_____	_____
operate	immerse
_____	_____

How did you do?

Even more /shuns/

Look at how the root words change when **ssion** or **cian** is added.

music – musician   discuss – discussion
physics – physician   submit – submission

Write rules to help you know which suffix to use.

If a word ends in_____, we should_____.

If a word ends in_____, we should_____.

Use your rules to add **ssion** or **cian** to these root words, writing out the new word in full.

magic	express
_____	_____
possess	optic
_____	_____
electric	permit
_____	_____
impress	politics
_____	_____
profess	technic
_____	_____

How did you do?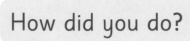

Sounds like /zhun/

Circle the /**zhun**/ sounding words, and write them on the television screen.

Sometimes **sion** makes a /**zhun**/ sound, such as in the word 'version'.

division   extension   conclusion   revision   pension   decision
suspension   explosion   invasion   comprehension

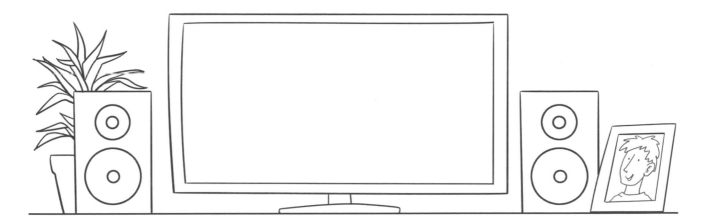

Choose the right words to complete the sentences.

1. Multiplication is the opposite of _____.

2. The bomb made a huge _____.

3. We made the _____ to stay an extra day.

4. In history, we learned about the Norman _____.

5. I came to the _____ she was right after all.

6. He needed to do lots of _____ before his exam.

How did you do?

More /zhun/ practice

Write the root words with the new suffix **sion**, then write a sentence for each word.

1. collide _____

_____

2. decide _____

_____

3. divert _____

_____

4. explode _____

_____

5. televise _____

_____

6. invade _____

_____

7. divide _____

_____

8. revise _____

_____

How did you do?

Recapping suffixes

Add the missing vowels to these **ation** words. Write the full word beside each.

1. cr__ __t__ __n   _____

2. f__rm__t__ __n   _____

3. __xp__ct__t__ __n   _____

4. g__n__r__t__ __n   _____

5. __bs__rv__t__ __n   _____

6. gr__d__ __t__ __n   _____

Add the suffix **tion**, **ation**, **sion** or **ssion** to complete the words.

found_____   permi_____   subtrac_____   divi_____

explan_____   exten_____

Look up these words in a dictionary and write their meanings.

generation _____

hesitation _____

submersion _____

precision _____

How did you do?

Recapping the suffix ous

Add **ous**, **ious**, **mous** or **lous** to complete the words. Write the whole word beside.

1. fabul_____   _____

2. poison_____   _____

3. myster_____   _____

4. ridicu_____   _____

5. prec_____   _____

6. grac_____   _____

7. miracu_____   _____

8. enor_____   _____

9. fabu_____   _____

10. gorge_____   _____

Circle the misspelled **ous** words, then write the correct spellings.

thunderus   delishus   hilarious   luxurios   generous

jealous   religous   serius   previos

_____   _____   _____

_____   _____

How did you do?

More suffix practice

Complete the words with **tion**, **sion**, **cian** or **ssion**.

confu_____   opti_____   percu_____

magi_____   competi_____   exten_____

corre_____   electri_____   profe_____

Find and circle the words from above in the word search.

i	o	c	r	p	e	r	s	c	i	o	n
p	r	o	f	e	s	s	i	o	n	p	i
n	t	r	a	r	t	y	s	n	i	t	h
o	l	r	e	c	u	s	t	f	o	i	n
i	k	e	m	u	g	i	a	u	d	c	i
s	s	c	u	s	e	w	g	s	b	i	m
n	e	t	a	s	u	i	n	i	s	a	t
e	x	i	t	i	p	o	i	o	h	n	y
t	b	o	z	o	u	i	a	n	o	i	s
x	h	n	l	n	a	i	c	i	g	a	m
e	l	e	c	t	r	i	c	i	a	n	o
e	c	o	m	p	e	t	i	t	i	o	n

How did you do?

45

Do you know your suffixes?

Add suffixes to complete the words.

Once there was a fam_____ mathemati_____. She was excellent

at addi_____, subtract_____, multiplic_____ and divi_____.

But her secret wish was to give up maths and become a

magi_____. She dreamed of appearing on televi_____ and was

really quite jea_____ when she saw others performing

marvel_____ tricks to perfec_____. She used her imagin_____

to pretend she had already begun her new occup_____, receiving

tremend_____ applause for her incredible illu_____s. Then her

chance finally came. There was to be a huge competi_____ to find

the best new act.

Write the words below, in the order they appear in the passage.

_____   _____

_____   _____

_____   _____

_____   _____

_____   _____

_____   _____

How did you do?

46

Suffix crossword

Use the words from the box to complete the crossword.

Each answer is a word with a suffix.

discussion   question   option   tremendous   education
gorgeous   tension   occupation   poisonous

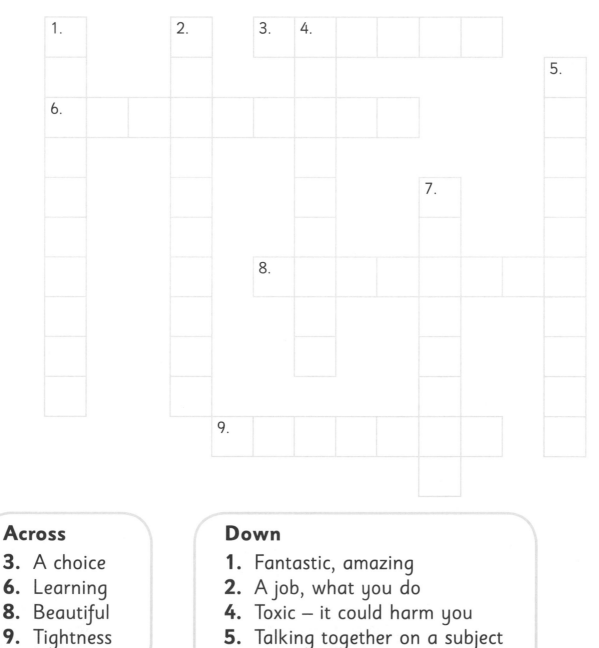

Across
3. A choice
6. Learning
8. Beautiful
9. Tightness

Down
1. Fantastic, amazing
2. A job, what you do
4. Toxic – it could harm you
5. Talking together on a subject
7. It needs an answer

How did you do?

Possession in singular nouns

Rewrite the phrases, using **'s** to show possession.

Use **'s** to show possession for singular nouns, like this: *Bob's hat is the hat belonging to Bob.*

1. the pen of the artist _____

2. the best in the world _____

3. the nest of the bird _____

4. the favourite of the nation _____

5. the choice of the customer _____

Rewrite this passage, making use of the possessive apostrophe for singular nouns.

The mother of Anna was annoyed when she went into the room of her daughter. The clothes of the girl were all over the floor. The shoes of Anna nearly tripped her up. The doors of the wardrobe were wide open. Jack, the older brother of Anna, stood in the doorway laughing. "The room of my sister is even worse than mine!" he said.

_____

_____

_____

_____

_____

_____

How did you do?

Possession in regular plurals (1)

Write the possessive nouns in the right shape.

> For regular plurals, we use an apostrophe after the final **s** to show possession, like this – horses' hooves.

apple's pips   cats' claws   pupils' results   rainbow's end
parents' evening   athlete's training   flags' designs
dog's owners   shapes' edges

Singular	Plural

Rewrite these phrases as plural possessives in a sentence.

1. tables legs _____

2. drawers contents _____

3. estate agents houses _____

4. teams tactics _____

How did you do?

Possession in regular plurals (2)

Plural nouns ending in **es** also use a final apostrophe to show possession, such as: *boxes' corners.*

Choose pairs of words from each bag to create plural possessives. Write them using the possessive apostrophe. Make two sets of phrases, a sensible one and a silly one. One is done to help you.

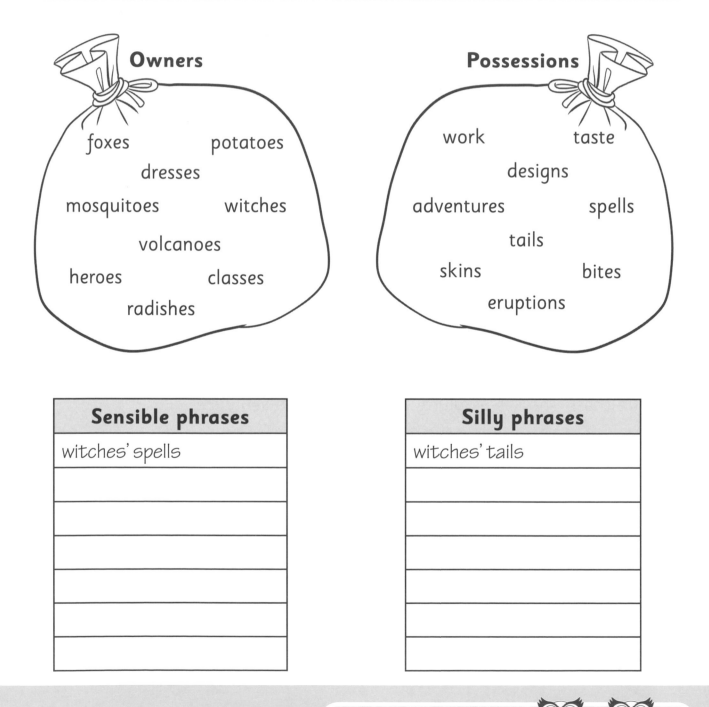

Owners

foxes   potatoes
     dresses
mosquitoes   witches
     volcanoes
heroes   classes
     radishes

Possessions

work   taste
     designs
adventures   spells
     tails
skins   bites
     eruptions

Sensible phrases
witches' spells

Silly phrases
witches' tails

How did you do?

Possession in irregular plurals (1)

Follow these rules for nouns with irregular plurals, to show possession.

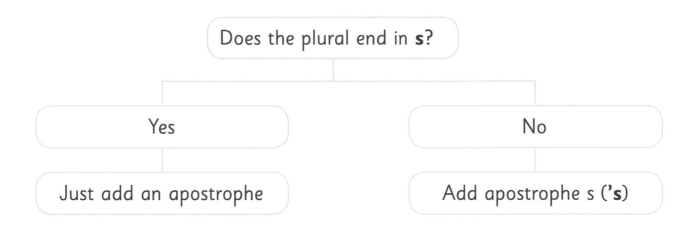

Does the plural end in **s**?

Yes | No

Just add an apostrophe | Add apostrophe s (**'s**)

Write the possessive forms of these plural nouns.

men		babies	
people		daisies	
elves		women	
ladies		countries	
mice		leaves	
children		fungi	
geese		cities	
shelves		fairies	

How did you do?

Possession in irregular plurals (2)

Rewrite these sentences as plurals. The first one has been done for you.

1. The fairy's wand was broken.

The fairies' wands were broken.

2. The buffalo's horn was a beautiful curvy shape.

_____

3. The cow recognised her calf's call.

_____

4. The cherry's juice tasted delicious.

_____

5. The child's school report was excellent.

_____

6. There was fresh straw in the pony's stable.

_____

7. The gallery's exhibition was magnificent.

_____

8. The lily's perfume filled the room.

_____

How did you do?

Plural or possessive? (1)

Circle the possessive nouns. Then write each word in the correct box.

Remember, the apostrophe shows possession.

myths   antiques   competition's   tongue's   televisions'

wolves'   magician's   choirs'   sleighs'   adventures   women's

admissions   scientists   couple's   picture's

Plurals	Singular Possessives	Plural Possessives

Choose the correct words to complete the sentences.

1. The _____ received praise for their groundbreaking discovery.

2. The _____ distant howls echoed through the forest.

3. It was hard to judge all the _____ excellent performances.

4. At the _____ close, Henri was declared the winner.

5. The _____ purposes are to detect taste and help us to swallow.

How did you do?

53

Plural or possessive? (2)

Write three sentences for each noun – one as a plural, one as a singular possessive and one as a plural possessive.

Common nouns can be used as plurals or as possessives.

duck   There were four ducks on the pond.

The duck's webbed feet left prints in the mud.

I heard the ducks' quacking across the farmyard.

pyramid

musician

creature

How did you do?

Possessive pronouns and the possessive apostrophe (1)

> We use pronouns in place of names. These are possessive pronouns: **mine**, **ours**, **yours**, **hers**, **his**, **theirs**.

Choose a possessive pronoun to complete each sentence.

1. This is my dinner and that one over there is _____.

2. Shabana's front door is red. Kate and Alex live down the street. _____ is green.

3. We won the relay race! The trophy is _____.

4. Sarah's sister claimed the shoes were _____.

5. I had to admit, the fault was all _____.

Using pronouns helps to avoid repetition. Underline words where you could use possessive pronouns. Write the correct pronoun that would replace them.

1. Jamie left home without his keys, but Simon had Simon's keys.

   _____

2. We went to the reception to collect our keys to the caravan. Dad asked which caravan was our caravan. _____

3. Bella wouldn't let Maddie wear her shoes. Bella said the shoes were Bella's. _____

How did you do?

More on possession

Unlike possessive nouns, possessive pronouns never use an apostrophe.

Write the words in the correct shape.

mine   Arthur's   theirs   hers   electricians'
puppies'   yours   league's   Egypt's   ours

Possessive nouns	Possessive pronouns

Rewrite these sentences, using **its**.

1. In autumn, the tree lost the tree's leaves.

_____

2. The lamb kept close to the lamb's mother.

_____

3. The racing driver's car lost the car's power.

_____

4. Slowly, the bonfire began to lose the bonfire's heat.

_____

How did you do?

Homophones (1)

Homophones are words that sound the same (or almost the same) but have different meanings and spellings.

Write the correct homophones to complete the sentences.

1. **ball/bawl** The baby began to _____ when it lost its _____.

2. **accept/except** I will _____ your offer _____ for one thing.

3. **affect/effect** My fall had a big _____. It began to _____ my confidence.

4. **mist/missed** Because of the _____ we _____ our turning.

5. **scene/seen** We had never _____ such a beautiful _____.

6. **weather/whether** _____ the _____ is fine or not, we will go to the beach.

Choose from **rain**, **rein** or **reign** to complete these sentences.

7. I hope it doesn't _____ on my birthday.

8. The Queen's _____ began in 1952.

Sometimes three words can be homophones.

9. You use a _____ to control a horse.

Now, select from **he'll**, **heel** and **heal**.

10. "Your wound will soon _____," the nurse said.

How did you do?

More homophones

You won't need to use all the words, so choose carefully!

Choose the correct homophone to complete this historic report.

medals/meddles	weather/whether	rain/rein/reign	sea/see
whose/who's	scene/seen	missed/mist	hear/here
affect/effect	great/grate	would/wood	
accept/except	wait/weight		

I was lucky enough to witness the coronation of Queen Elizabeth II,

_____ long _____ began more than 60 years ago. It was

a truly _____ occasion, despite the poor _____. A fine

_____ turned into quite heavy _____, but this didn't

_____ the crowd's excitement. After a long _____ I could

_____ the troops of mounted horsemen coming nearer. All the

soldiers marching by, proudly wore their _____. And then came

the Queen in her golden coach. What an unforgettable _____!

It had such an emotional _____ on everyone. We all cheered;

some even cried! (_____ that is, for one little girl, who had

fallen asleep!) I _____ not have _____ it for anything.

How did you do?

Even more homophones!

Some of the homophones in this passage are incorrect. Underline the mistakes and write the correct words in the grid, in the order they appear in the passage.

Once upon a time their were four bares – two pears of twins. One pare were groan-up bears and the other pair were quite young. The youngsters could not weight to be older. They wood count the days on there tiny pause, hoping that soon they would be big. But the adults said "What's the hurry? Just except what you are and enjoy yourself." And off they went, for a bit of piece.

"It's all very well for them," said one of the youngsters. "They can do what they want."

"So can we!" said his twin, and off he zoomed, arms outstretched, pretending to be a plain. He made so much noise, the adults herd him. "That young bear is effecting my nap," said one of them. "Heal have to stop!" So he hid behind a tree, and as the little bear past by, he court him in his grate big paws. "I know I said enjoy yourself," he said with a grown, "but please, will you do it somewhere else?"

How did you do?

Tricky words

Sort these tricky words according to how many syllables they have.

accidentally   believe   breathe   century   disappear

eighth   favourite   grammar   guard   island   knowledge

naughty   occasionally   possession   pressure   separate

One syllable	Two syllables	Three syllables	Five syllables

Write words from the table that fit these definitions.

1. We must do this to stay alive. _____

2. The rules for how to use language. _____

3. To have faith that something is true. _____

4. To do something by mistake. _____

5. To set something apart. _____

6. The position after seventh. _____

How did you do?

More tricky words

Find the words to solve the clues.

> accidentally   believe   bicycle   centre   eighth   enough   fruit
> group   height   medicine   pressure   special   weight

1. Which four words spell the /**s**/ sound differently?

    _____ _____ _____ _____

2. Which word spells the /**ee**/ sound differently?

    _____

3. Which two words spell the /**sh**/ sound differently?

    _____ _____

4. Which two words spell the /**oo**/ sound differently?

    _____ _____

5. Which two words spell the /**ay**/ sound differently?

    _____ _____

6. Which word spells the /**igh**/ sound differently?

    _____

7. Which word spells the /**f**/ sound differently?

    _____

How did you do?

Even more tricky words!

Read the passage and underline the ten spelling mistakes.

It is dificult to discribe just how inportant science is to our lives. Without the ecksperiments scientists perform, many things we take for granted would not exist. Even in the 21st sentury, for example, new medisens are being made. In their laboratories, scientists sometimes have to seperate microscopic parts of a substance in order to use it to create a new materiel. It's hard to imajin where we would be without their specialist nolidje.

Write the correct spellings below, in the order they appear in the passage.

How did you do?

Dictionary skills

Read this advert and circle all the spelling mistakes. Check them in a dictionary. Then write the correct spelling in the grid and the page number of the dictionary where you found it.

The County
ORKESTRA

Vacancy

The County orkestra has a vacancy for a new musition. We need someone who can play both the piano and the klarinette. This could be a great opertunerty for the right candydayt. We enjoy entering compertishons which are treemendus fun. If you beleeve you have the right kwolificasions and want to be part of our exciting fewcher, then apply today!

Correct spelling	Dictionary page number	Correct spelling	Dictionary page number

How did you do?

Meanings in context

Read this extract from the story of Robin Hood. Underline any words you do not know or fully understand. Try to work out what the words mean using clues in the sentence or other parts of the story. Then find the words in a dictionary and complete the grid below.

According to folklore, Robin Hood was a legendary renegade and accomplished archer who reputedly robbed the rich and gave to the poor. Despite allegedly living in medieval times, he is still renowned today. The truth about him has been debated for centuries and stories of his daring exploits were sung about in ancient ballads. Some scholars believe Robin was the Earl of Huntingdon, while other academics contend that he hailed from Yorkshire. But he is usually associated with Nottingham where his principal foe was the despicable Sheriff.

Unknown word	What I think it means	Dictionary definition	Was I right? ✓or ✗

How did you do?

Spellchecker

Max has underlined the words he knows he has misspelled. Look them up in a dictionary and write the correct words for him in the grid below.

Dear Auntie Flossie,

I can't thank you <u>enuff</u> for the <u>brillyent</u> present! How did you know <u>arkeology</u> was my <u>pashion</u>? (<u>Ackcherlly</u> I <u>gess</u> you asked Mum and Dad!) <u>Obviusly</u>, I'm just an <u>amater</u> at the moment, but with such great tools, I'll soon be as good as the <u>proffessionals</u>! Any time you fancy an <u>arkeologicle</u> dig in your garden, just let me know!

Thanks a million!

Love,

Max

Misspelled word	Dictionary spelling	Dictionary page number
enuff		
brillyent		
arkeology		
pashion		
ackcherly		
gess		
obviusly		
amater		
proffessionals		
arkeologicle		

How did you do?

Extend your dictionary skills

When words begin with the same letter, we use the second or third letter to find them in the dictionary.

Write these words in alphabetical order in the grid below.

magician   medicine   marvellous   musician   mechanic
millionaire   multiplication   myth   mountainous   mystery
misbehave   measure   machine   material   mention

How did you do?

More dictionary work

Use the second and third letters of the words below to find them in a dictionary. Circle the correct meaning in the table and write the page number where you found the word.

Word	Meaning 1	Meaning 2	Dictionary page number
illegible	Too difficult to read.	A shelf that is not level.	
irrepressible	Not bouncy or springy.	Unable to be stopped.	
footing	Alternative name for football.	A building's foundation.	
amendment	An alteration or change.	To remember.	
laudable	Worthy of praise.	Extremely loud.	
portfolio	List of ships in a port.	Collection of work.	
smoulder	Burn slowly without flames.	An elderly person.	
gullible	Greedy and aggressive like a gull.	Easily fooled into thinking something.	
mistletoe	An infection of the foot.	A plant with white berries.	
nauseous	Feeling sick.	A type of animal which chews on wood.	
timorous	Easily scared.	Made of wood.	

How did you do?

Glossaries

Glossaries are mini-dictionaries that give the meanings of words in a non-fiction book.

Use a dictionary to find the meaning of these words that might appear in the glossary of a recipe book. If words have more than one meaning, choose the one that sounds like it might be from a recipe book.

boil	
broil	
clarify	
dissolve	
fillet	
garnish	
knead	
marinate	
poach	
whip	

How did you do?

Missing vowels

The vowels are missing from these tricky words. Write the full words, putting in the missing vowels.

1. __cc__d__nt__lly _____

2. ___ ___ghth _____

3. b__s__n__ss _____

4. f__v__ __r__t__ _____

5. p__rt__c__l__r _____

6. q__ __st__ __n _____

7. __lth__ __gh _____

8. c__nt__ry _____

9. p__t__t__ __s _____

10. b__l__ __v__ _____

11. s__p__r__t__ _____

12. n__ __ghty _____

13. F__br__ __ry _____

14. c__ __ght _____

15. kn__wl__dg__ _____

How did you do?

Tricky word search

Circle each tricky word in the word search below.

believe   bicycle   breathe   calendar   centre
describe   disappear   imagine   probably
separate   special   opposite

e	b	o	l	e	t	i	s	o	p	p	o
d	i	c	t	d	u	p	s	l	i	o	n
i	c	a	l	e	n	d	a	r	s	e	a
s	y	m	b	s	o	c	e	n	t	r	e
a	c	h	r	c	i	s	m	e	l	k	e
p	l	o	p	r	o	b	a	b	l	y	n
p	e	r	t	i	k	e	w	o	a	b	i
e	z	e	a	b	o	u	l	t	i	m	g
a	i	u	b	e	r	n	d	o	c	l	a
r	u	b	b	e	l	i	e	v	e	y	m
i	e	e	h	t	a	e	r	b	p	r	i
s	e	p	a	r	a	t	e	l	s	y	s

How did you do?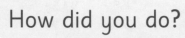

Chopping up words

Chopping words into syllables or chunks helps you remember how to spell them, like this: **in/ten/tion/ally** or **inten/tion/ally** or **intention/ally**.

Show two ways to chop up each of these words.

purposefully   _____   _____

ungenerous   _____   _____

mystical   _____   _____

interpretation   _____   _____

subterranean   _____   _____

adventurous   _____   _____

unforgettable   _____   _____

questionable   _____   _____

peculiarly   _____   _____

How did you do?

Using what you know

You can use the spellings you know to help you spell longer words. For example, if you can spell **sign** you can use it to spell **signal** and **signature**.

Use these root words to make new words. The root words don't have to be at the beginning. Check your spellings in a dictionary.

comic _____   music _____   action _____

friend _____   place _____   connect _____

person _____   rest _____   machine _____

How did you do?

Looking for patterns

Grouping words that are similar in some ways can help you to spell them.

Choose ways to group these tricky words and explain why you grouped them that way on the line below.

although	answer	breathe	business	certain	early
earth	eighth	exercise	increase	island	knowledge
naughty	notice	particular	peculiar	recent	regular

How did you do?

Sentences with prefixes

Write six sentences. Use at least one word from both lists in each sentence.

Words with prefixes	Plural possessives
disappointed	animals'
impatient	artists'
imperfect	children's
incorrect	mice's
international	ponies'
irresponsible	Romans'
reappeared	women's
supermarket	

_____

_____

_____

_____

_____

_____

_____

_____

_____

How did you do?

Opening paragraph

Write the opening paragraph of a story set in the future. Include:

- some words with the suffixes **ly**, **ous**, **tion** and **sion**
- some possessive pronouns, such as **theirs**, **whose** and **his**
- some words with the /**s**/ sound spelt **sc**.

Note your ideas in the table below before you write your paragraph.

My characters	My suffix words	My possessive plurals	My /sc/ words

_____

_____

_____

_____

_____

_____

How did you do?

Making sentences

Write sentences that include a noun, adjective, verb and adverb from the lists below. You may change singulars to plurals and alter verb tenses if you wish.

Nouns	Adjectives	Verbs	Adverbs
antique	young	groan	completely
Egypt	poisonous	disagree	usually
superman	ordinary	fascinate	angrily
autograph	popular	obey	happily
creature	tremendous	affect	gently
chemist	obvious	disappear	frantically

_____

_____

_____

_____

_____

_____

_____

_____

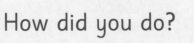

How did you do?

Spot the mistakes

This builder has written a letter to try to get a job, but is unlikely to be successful as there are many mistakes in it! Underline the mistakes and then write the correct word in the grid below.

Hear are my ideas for your kitchen reefurbishment. I suggest you replace your single cupboards with dubble one's and install a sentral iland such as profesional shefs' use. This would give you a large preparashun area. Ortomatic appliances would be included as standard.
We can also offer suggeschuns for replacement furnicher. Before you decide weather to except my plans, you may like to talk with your nayber, who has used our service's before.

How did you do?

Correct the errors

Help this advertiser by underlining the mistakes in her advert before it goes into the newspaper. Rewrite the advertisement correctly on the lines below.

FOR SAIL

A collecshun of anteek meddles.

These include meddles from varius countries so are of intanashunal intrest. All are in perfect condision. This fasinating groop of historic item's will be of grate intrest to collectors' of military artefacts or anyone whose intrested in histori. This is such an extraordinary collechsun that it is dificult to discribe briefly. If you wish to learn more about them, please contact me at the adres below, menshuning this advert.

_____

_____

_____

_____

_____

_____

_____

_____

How did you do?

Proofreading

Read through this notice carefully, circling the mistakes and writing the corrections above, then listing them in the grid in the order that they appear in the article.

Notise of closure

Areas of this service stasion will be closed next weekend in order that inportant maintenance work can be carried out, resulting in limitid facilities. Unfortunatly this will innclude both the mens' and ladie's toilets, but temporary toilets will be available in the car park. Speshul arrangements will be in place for dissabled customers. This work will not effect our shops but altho the café will be closed, extra drinks masheens will be provided near the childrens' play area.

We hope this does not cause too much disconvenience.

How did you do?

Progress chart

Colour in Ollie when you have completed the chapter.

1 — Revisit and reinforce

2 — Prefixes

3 — Suffixes and word endings

6 — Applying and using knowledge

5 — Building knowledge

4 — Possession

CONGRATULATIONS!

Name: ....

You have completed the

Spelling and vocabulary Workbook

AGES 8–9

Age: ....   **Date:** ....